Guide to Private Placement Project FundingTrade Programs

Understanding High-Level Project Funding Trade Programs

SIR PATRICK BIJOU

All Rights Reserved Sir Patrick Bijou. This is not an offer to sell or buy instruments or other securities. It contains only generalized information for the education of the reader.

The intellectual rights to this book is hereby owned by Sir Patrick Bijou and no part of this book can be copied or transmitted without his express consent.

© copyright Sir Patrick Bijou 2018

ABOUT THE AUTHOR

Like never before, the accomplishment of a business relies upon how well you draw with clients and construct positive encounters. This at last results in a solid brand dependability. Sir Patrick is a dynamic Investment banker, Fund Manager, and REDEMPTION JUDGE for the International Court of Justice and International Criminal Courts, he is also a published Author.

As a notable investment banker, he has also worked on Wall Street, a very capable and highly experienced trader in the derivative and bond markets, having setup MTN desks within Lloyds Bank. Sir Patrick's journey into content writing has allowed him to become an exceptionally motivated and enthusiastic author and professional communicator. Experienced in both proactive campaign-driven and responsive communications.

He has been responsible for serving large corporates, the creation of new credit for international supply chains and SMEs, public sector, and clients across a range of products that include supply chain finance, receivable finance, contract monetization and a broad range of trade services. Sir Patrick undertook similar roles at Conduit Capital and Morgan Stanley. His extensive contacts are with major banks around the world and include Wells Fargo, HSBC, and BNP Paribas where he deals at board level. Today, he determines it is right to take this concept to the next level and help others free their full business potential.

Sir Patrick has tailored funding and investments for many different clients including governments, banks and financial institutions, and has implemented over $1.3B funding for social housing.

Coming together is a beginning, keeping together is progress, and working together is a success"

Thank you for reading this book and please write a review.

BOOK DESCRIPTION

This book teaches the secret that few will ever know that have deliberately been kept private. Learning about a financial construction that will allow you to earn profits much more than the banks' ability to pay.

The Internet is filled with liars, cheats and thieves, all spreading misinformation which have resulted in many potential investors being burned so many times. Fortunately, luck, persistence and solid relationships with over 35 years in banking has found the author a winning formula and panacea for the secret to legitimate trading programs dispelling the myths of its existence. This book will ensure that you do not waste time sifting through the flotsam the Internet brings, but provides a clear and concise guide into the mysterious world of Private Placement and High Yield Investment opportunities. It is a must-read short guide of knowledge required to learn all about managed buy sell programs its history, its future, and the people that are allowed to join this illustrious and exclusive club for making money. The Secret is now being revealed to those who care to know and the reality of how true wealth is created just for a few. Enjoy the journey, it will open your eyes!

GUIDE TO PRIVATE PLACEMENT TRADE PROGRAMS

Understanding High-Level Project Funding Trade Programs As A Prospective Client

This is not an offer to sell or solicit securities. This book is for general information purposes only, and is not to be construed as solicitation. This document is provided upon request for informational use only. The information contained within is based on relationships with providers in the international banking world where these operate.

SIR PATRICK BIJOU

Table of Contents

INTRODUCTION...1

CHAPTER 1 - INTRODUCTION...6

CHAPTER 2 - THE BASIC REASONS FOR THIS KIND OF TRADE PROGRAM...9

CHAPTER 3 - WHO CAN PARTICIPATE?............................16

CHAPTER 4 - COMPLIANCE AND DUE DILIGENCE...........17

CHAPTER 4 - WHAT DOES "DUE DILIGENCE" MEAN?......22

CHAPTER 4 - START THE CONVERSATION WITH THE PROVIDER...24

CHAPTER 5 - THE SUBMISSION..25

CHAPTER 6 - TIMELINES..26

CHAPTER 7 - HOW IS MY MONEY PROTECTED FROM LOSS...29

CHAPTER 8 - SUMMARY...30

APPENDIX...32

CLIENT INFORMATION SHEET..33

CORPORATE RESOLUTION – IF APPLICABLE..................40

PASSPORT..43

PROOF OF FUNDS...44

INTRODUCTION

Decades ago at the end of World War II, the financial underpinnings of most of the countries in the world were devastated by the costs of fighting - and then rebuilding- infrastructures and other critical projects needed for reviving and sustaining humanity.

A plan was devised that encompassed various strategies to create funding for these projects which, by their nature, were not meant to create business ventures that would be profitable in the purest sense of the capitalist world. Reconstructed roads, bridges, hospitals, and other infrastructure needs are not the best investment when a capitalist is seeking a return on his or her investment from ordinary startup and operation.

> *Today's financial and economic needs have grown in orders of magnitude over the last 40 years*

To help entice private money to create funding for desperately needed projects, the financial and political engineers of this plan created a way for wealthy families and corporations holding enormous sums of cash and certain other assets to invest and achieve profits from buying and selling bank paper, profiting handsomely, and dedicating the bulk of the profits into needed projects.

This white paper is not meant to go in details of how all of this transpired, nor is it meant to be a complete education in this tight, niche financing scheme. It is, years however, helpful to have an understanding of how things got started and have evolved into the ongoing buying, selling or trading of bank paper (medium term notes, debentures, bonds, guarantees, etc.) as a method of generating profits, the majority of which would be mostly used to fund the reconstruction and rebuilding around the globe.

Today's financial and economic needs have grown in orders of magnitude over the last 40+ years, with the increasing worldwide poverty, starvation, ignorance and illiteracy, plus the continuing needs of a government to provide basic services for its citizens. The post-World War II system of funding still supports the reasons for providing comparatively handsome profits to the client, whilst at the same time designating the majority of those profits to pay for these needed projects. Times have changed, the names of the instruments are different, and the manners in which they generate profits have changed, but the core objective is still the same: To fund environmental and humanitarian projects around the globe.

There is indeed, a tremendous amount more detail than can be disclosed here. But the purpose of this document is to help you become aware of the opportunity and the reasons why it is in existence. You can find the details in various places by researching the Internet and consulting with knowledgeable professionals. Most finance, accounting, and general banking people have no idea that this exists, and even greater disbelief when hearing of the profit that are generated. Ask any CPA, Attorney, and Banker (other than the senior level management of the bank) about these programs, and they will generally be completely unaware, or highly suspicious, of this. While good people, the level of education in this arena is far greater and beyond their training and expertise.

These are considered PRIVATE PLACEMENTS. This information is tightly controlled, and anyone seeking to learn more by calling the banks or asking the government agencies will be told there is no such thing as this, and they will deny any more information. You will see why it must be this way, if this system is to succeed behind the scenes to advance humanity and our environment, as well as provide attractive profits for those with the money.

> PRIVATE PLACEMENT is an umbrella term that covers all types of transactions that are not meant for the general public to know about. That's why they are PRIVATE. In general, all types of financial offerings that are not public are private, and reserved for those with the proper financial and background qualifications.

I created this book to help prospective readers who are unfamiliar with the Project Funding Trade Program arena. After years plowing through the thousands of "Internet Brokers" who are not truly connected to anyone who is able to perform, and then ultimately becoming associated with the actual performers, I developed this book to answer questions coming from a place of knowledge learned over several years. I present this to you as a means of clearing up the many misunderstandings that people around the globe have about these, and to provide some insight into the funding of major infrastructure, humanitarian and environmental projects that will benefit humanity.

First, let's clear up what the term "Private Placement" really means.

PRIVATE PLACEMENT is an umbrella term that covers all types of transactions that are not meant for a general public to know about. That's why they are PRIVATE. Think of Limited Partnerships, Stock and Bond offerings, etc. as all falling into this generic term PPP.

To clarify this, think of a Private Placement Program as ANYTHING NOT BEING OFFERED TO THE PUBLIC.

Somewhere along the way, the term also became used to describe certain trade programs. When used in the context of Project Funding Trade Programs, which is the topic we are covering here, the term PPP is synonymous with Project Funding Trade Programs, sometimes also referred to as Managed Buy/Sells, which is also another type of trading activity that more financial people would think of.

As you read this I hope you will gain a better understanding of the specific Project Funding Trade Program system. As a prospective new client, you will naturally have additional questions.

You will walk through the initial steps described here, and see why certain information cannot be revealed until you have been cleared through the necessary due diligence process.

Remember that these programs operate at a very high level in the banking industry—a level where very few bank executives have knowledge. Asking a branch manager about these, or even at the Senior Vice President level, will generally result in blank stares, or "we don't do that" answers. Bank secrecy. Or just not being "in the loop" at their bank.

It is sad that the Internet has created such a cacophony of people who have confused, confounded, and conspired to work fraudulently, mainly because the amounts of money we talk about here are, for many, inconceivable. Exaggeration of profits, program availabilities and other outright misinformation (purposefully or ignorantly) has caused so many legitimate investors to huddle up inside their shells. If I hadn't had the education I have received, I would do the same thing.

Being on the provider side, we see similar problems brought on by incompetence, cheating and lying, not just by intermediaries surprisingly enough, but also by would-be clients. Unfortunately, people often pose as the owner of the bank account, only for it to be discovered this isn't the case.

It is my hope that this information will provide a bit more clarity, and help you better understand the process, which isn't all that complicated once you understand the moving parts.

CHAPTER 1 - INTRODUCTION

Decades ago, at the end of World War II, the financial foundation of most of the countries involved in the war were devastated by the costs of fighting -- and then rebuilding-- infrastructure and other critical projects needed for reviving and sustaining humanity.

A plan was devised that encompassed various strategies to create funding for these projects which, by their nature, were not meant at the time to create business ventures that would be profitable in the purest sense of the capitalist world. Reconstructed roads, bridges, hospitals, and infrastructure needs are not the best investment when a capitalist is seeking a return on his or her investment from ordinary startup and operation.

To help attract private money to create funding for desperately needed projects, the financial and political engineers of this plan created a way for wealthy families and corporations holding enormous sums of cash and certain other assets to invest and achieve profits from buying and selling bank paper, profiting handsomely, and dedicating the bulk of the profits into needed projects.

This white paper is not meant to go in details of how all of this transpired, nor is it meant to be a complete education in this tight, niche financing scheme. It is, however, helpful to have an understanding of how things got started and have evolved into the ongoing buying, selling or trading of bank paper (medium term notes, debentures, bonds, guarantees, etc.) as a method of generating profits, the majority of which would be mostly used to fund the reconstruction and rebuilding around the globe.

Today's financial and economic needs have grown in orders of magnitude over the last 40+ years, with increasing worldwide poverty, starvation, ignorance and illiteracy, plus the continuing needs of a government to provide infrastructure and services for its citizens. The post-World War II system of funding still supports the reasons for providing comparatively handsome profits to the client, whilst at the same time designating the majority of those profits to pay for these needed projects.

Times have changed, the names of the instruments used in trade are different, and the manners in which they generate profits have changed, but the core objective is still the same: To fund environmental and humanitarian projects around the globe.

There is indeed, a tremendous amount more detail than this document will cover. But the purpose of this document is to help you become aware and educated about this specialized and unique form of trading, and the reasons why it is in existence.

Most finance, accounting, and general banking people have no idea that this exists, and d i s p l a y even greater disbelief when hearing of the profit that are generated. Ask any CPA, Attorney, and Banker (other than the senior level management of the bank) about these programs, and they will generally be completely unaware, or highly suspicious, of this. While good people, the level of education in this arena is far greater and beyond their training and expertise.

These are considered PRIVATE in every sense of the word. This information is tightly controlled, and anyone seeking to learn more by calling the banks or asking the government agencies will be told there is no such thing as this, and they will deny any more information. You will see why it must be this way, if this system is to succeed behind the scenes to advance humanity and our environment, as well as provide attractive profits for those with the money.

CHAPTER 2 - THE BASIC REASONS FOR THIS KIND OF TRADE PROGRAM

First and foremost, these trade programs exist to "create" money. Money is created by creating debt.

For example: You as an individual can agree to loan $100 to a friend, with the understanding that the interest for the loan will be 10%, resulting in a total to be repaid of $110. What you have done is to actually create $10, even though you don't see that money initially.

For the moment, don't consider the regulatory and legal aspects of such an agreement, just the numbers. Banks are doing this sort of lending every day, but with much more money. Essentially, banks have the power to create money from nothing. Since PPP's involve trading with discounted bank-issued debt instruments, money is created due to the fact that such instruments are deferred payment obligations, or debts. Money is created from that debt.

Theoretically, any person, company, or organization can issue debt notes (again, ignore the legalities of the process). Debt notes are deferred payment liabilities.

Example: A person (individual, company, or organization) is in need of $100. He generates a debt note for $120 that matures after 1 year, and sells this debt for $100. This process is known as "discounting". Theoretically, the issuer is able to issue as many such debt notes at whatever face value he desires – as long as borrowers believe that he's financially strong enough to honor them upon maturity.

Debts notes such as Medium Terms Notes (MTN), Bank Guarantees (BG), and Standby Letters of Credit (SBLC) are issued at discounted prices by major world banks in the billions every day. Essentially, they "create" such debt notes out of thin air, merely by creating a document.

The core problem: To issue such a debt note is very simple, but the issuer would have problems finding Clients unless the buyer "believes" that the issuer is financially strong enough to honor that debt note upon maturity. Any bank can issue such a debt note, sell it at discount, and promise to pay back the full-face value at the time the debt note matures. But would that issuing bank be able to find any buyer for such a debt note without being financially strong?

If one of the largest banks in Western Europe sold debt notes with a face value of €1M EURO at a discounted price of €800,000, most individuals would consider purchasing one, given the issuing bank's financial reputation and means, along with the ability to verify it beforehand. Conversely, if a stranger approached an individual on the street with an identical bank note, issued by an unknown bank, and offered it for the same sale price; most people would never consider that offer. It is a matter of trust and credibility. This also illustrates why there's so much fraud and so many bogus instruments in this business.

LARGE DEBTS' INSTRUMENTS' MARKET

As a consequence of the previous statements, there is an enormous daily market of discounted bank instruments involving issuing banks, the trade groups, and the groups of exit-Clients (Pension Funds, large financial institutions, etc.) in an exclusive Private Placement arena.

All such activities by the bank are done as "Off-Balance Sheet Activities". As such, the bank benefits in many ways. Off-Balance Sheet Activities are contingent assets and liabilities, where the value depends upon the outcome of which the claim is based, similar to that of an option. Off-Balance Sheet Activities appear on the balance sheet ONLY as memoranda items. When they generate a cash flow they appear as a credit or debit in the balance sheet. The bank does not have to consider binding capital constraints, as there is no deposit liability.

NORMAL STOCKS AND BONDS TRADING VS. PRIVATE PLACEMENT

All trading programs in the Private Placement arena involve trade with such discounted debt notes in some fashion. Further, in order to avoid the legal restrictions, this trading can only be done on a private level. This is the main difference between this type of trading and "normal" trading, which is highly regulated by most countries. This is a Private Placement level business transaction that is free from the usual restrictions present in the securities market.

Usually, trading is performed under the "open market" (also known as the "spot market") where discounted instruments are bought and sold with auction-type bids. To participate in such trading, the traders must be in full control of the funds, otherwise they lack the means buy the instruments and resell them. Also, there are fewer arbitrage transactions in this market, since all participants have knowledge of the instruments and their prices.

However, in addition to the open market there is a closed, private market wherein lies a restricted number of "master commitment holders". These holders are Trusts with huge amounts of money that enter contractual agreements with banks to buy newly issued instruments at a specific price during an allotted period of time. Their job is to resell these instruments, so they contract sub-commitment holders, who in turn contract exit-Clients.

These programs are all based on arbitrage transactions with pre-defined prices. As such, the traders never need to be in control of the client's funds. However, no program can start unless there is a sufficient quantity of money backing each transaction. It is at this point the clients are needed, because the involved banks and commitment holders are not allowed to trade with their own money unless they have reserved enough funds on the market, comprising unused money that belongs to clients, never at risk.

The trading banks can loan money to the traders. Typically, this money is loaned at a ratio of 1:10, but during certain conditions this ratio can be as high as 20:1. In other words, if the trader can "reserve" $100M, then the bank can loan $1B. In all actuality, the bank is giving the trader a line of credit based on how much money the trader or commitment holder has, since the banks won't loan that much money without collateral, no matter how much money the clients have.

Because bankers and financial experts who are not privy to this but are well aware of the open market, and equally aware of the so-called "MTN-programs", but are closed out of the private market, they find it hard to believe it is possible or that it exists. Ignorance is absolutely encouraged because of the very sensitive nature.

ARBITRAGE AND LEVERAGE

Private Placement trading safety is based on the fact that the transactions are performed as arbitrage transactions. This means that the instruments will be bought and resold immediately with pre-defined prices. A number of Clients and sellers are contracted, including exit-Clients comprising mostly of large financial institutions, insurance companies, or extremely wealthy individuals.

The issued instruments are never sold directly to the exit-buyer, but to a chain of clients. For obvious reasons the involved banks cannot directly participate in these transactions, but are still profiting from it indirectly by loaning money with interest to the trader or client as a line of credit. This is their leverage. Furthermore, the banks profit from the commissions involved in each transaction.

The client's principal does not have to be used for the transactions, as it is only reserved as a compensating balance ("mirrored") against this credit line. This credit line is then used to back up the arbitrage transactions. Since the trading is done as arbitrage, the money ("credit line") doesn't have to be used, but it must still be available to back up each and every transaction.

Such programs never fail because they don't begin before all actors have been contracted, and each actor knows exactly what role to play and how they will profit from the transactions. A trader who is able to secure this leverage is able to control a line of credit typically 10 to 20 times that of the principal. Even though the trader is in control of that money, the money still cannot be spent. The trader need only show that the money is under his control, and is not being used elsewhere at the time of the transaction.

This concept can be illustrated in the following example. Assume you are offered the chance to buy a car for $30,000 and that you also find another buyer that is willing to buy it from you for $35,000. If the transactions are completed at the same time, then you will not be required to "spend" the $30,000 and then wait to receive the $35,000. Performing the transactions at the same time nets you an immediate profit of $5,000. However, you must still have that $30,000 and prove it is under your control.

Arbitrage transactions with discounted bank instruments are done in a similar way. The involved traders never actually spend the money, but they must be in control of it. The client's principal is reserved directly for this, or indirectly in order for the trader to leverage a line of credit.

Confusion is common because most seem to believe that the money must be spent in order to complete the transaction. Even though this is the traditional way of trading - buy low and sell high – and also the common way to trade on the open market for securities and bank instruments, it is possible to set up legal arbitrage transactions if there is a chain of contracted Clients in place, and the trader can show he had the money in hand before he executed the first-round purchase. This is where your funds come into play, and you are rewarded handsomely.

This is why client funds blocked for use in a Project Funding Trade Programs are always safe without any trading risk: The trader is using the Client funds to obtain a credit line, which is what is used in his or her trading activities.

HIGH YIELD

Compared to the yield from traditional investments, these programs usually get a very high yield. A yield of 50%-100% per week is possible. Impossible, you say? Read on.

For example: Assume a leverage effect of 10:1, meaning the trader is able to back each buy-sell transaction with ten times the amount of money that the client has in his bank account. In other words, the client has €100M, and the trader is able to work with £€1B. Assume also the trader is able to complete three buy-sell transactions per week for 40 banking weeks (one year), with a 5% profit from each buy-sell transaction:

> (5% profit/transaction) (3 transactions/week)
> = 15% profit/week
> Assume 10x leverage effect = 150% profit...
> PER WEEK!

Even with a split of profit between the client and trading group, this still results in a double-digit weekly yield. This example can still be seen as conservative, since first tier trading groups can achieve a much higher single spread for each transaction, as well as a markedly higher number of weekly trades.

CHAPTER 3 - WHO CAN PARTICIPATE?

Believe it or not, having hundreds of millions, billions or trillions of dollars in your pocket does not automatically allow you entre' into a program. As much money as you may have available for this (and please remember, most programs require a 100,000,000 Euro cash to start), more important is the quality and caliber of your personality and cooperativeness in providing details about your situation. In other words, are you easy to work with, cooperative, and pleasant, or are you aggressive, complaining, and unwilling to do what is required?

If I were to describe the best client, it would be one who understands that without a good relationship of Trust, Honesty, Integrity, and Accountability and Understanding of each party's needs, nothing will ever happen. From the strength of a trusting relationship, transactions can proceed in a good way. When a client misrepresents him/herself in any way, it is always discovered in the due diligence, and that client ends up on a permanent list of disqualified individuals who are prohibited from trading.

Deal opportunities come and go every day. But the Relationship that lives on will bring forth new opportunities that fit your plans. Few people understand that, no matter how wealthy they are, and they are more often than not turned away at the beginning if they are difficult to work with.

CHAPTER 4 - COMPLIANCE AND DUE DILIGENCE

What does 'compliance' mean? Sadly, in this world of broker-jokers and other folks trying to explain what it means, the understanding, explanation and interpretations vary from one person to the next. If you think education is expensive, try ignorance! Simply, when someone says they need to run you through "compliance", that is short-hand for completing some basic due-diligence on you AND YOUR MONEY before engaging in a conversation. New Basel III regulations require each principal to "Know Your Customer" before engaging in the next steps. There are clients who insist that, for whatever reason, they are too important and 'well known' to have to provide this starting information. This is the fatal attitude that will stop a fledgling relationship dead in its tracks. For whatever reason—most likely they have been burned by Internet brokers who merely pass their information along without any real business relationship to a provider—the knee-jerk reaction is to not send anyone anything. Then, of course, they wonder why they cannot find a source at all!

SOLICITATION (FOR U.S. CLIENTS)

There are many definitions of Soliciting. The term solicitation is used in a variety of legal contexts. A person who asks someone to commit an illegal act has committed the criminal act of solicitation. Used in other contexts, non-solicitation may be part of an employment or contractor business agreement to prohibit a person from soliciting

Some believe non-solicitation is a Securities Exchange Commission (SEC) rule. After researching the SEC website (www.sec.gov) and speaking with knowledgeable people there, nowhere does it discuss non-solicitation in the context of this business. However, Licensed Broker/Dealers and certain other US Securities licensees may be regulated differently.

For the purpose of this particular business, *nonsolicitation may be the policy of the seller for their own reason, AS WELL as the legal ones.*

As a Client Prospect, if you want to do business with the provider, you start the ball rolling by making a specific request by providing the starting documents to make it through due diligence.

> *Remember, this is a " By-Invitation Only" business.*

The Provider's position is simple, but inflexible: The BUYER starts with his/her Request for a specific type of opportunity -- in writing. Since the Seller has the goods, this is, in many cases, their strict policy.

INITIAL DOCUMENTS FOR APPLICATION TO THE PROVIDER

1. A Client Information Sheet (CIS) with all of the blanks filled in. Your personal banker's information must be listed along with a main number for the bank and the banker's bank email address. Gmail and other non-bank-domain email accounts do not count.

2. A color copy of the Client's Passport

3. A Bank Statement showing an **available cash balance** of at least €100,000,000 (One Hundred Million Euro) free and clear and **not** blocked already. If the funds are already blocked, they do not qualify. Before you submit, have your bank **unblock** the funds first, and then provide the POF.

Together these constitute the Client making the first move. Let's call this Package 1: The Initial Application. It is your "Application" for being accepted as a Client who is financially and personally qualified. It is **not** the last document you will be asked for, but it is the key in the door that turns the lock to enter the trading domain.

Upon receipt of the above preliminary documents in Package 1, the Client is checked out at agencies such as Treasury, Homeland Security or the bank's governmental agencies (like FSA in the UK). If the buyer principal and his money are clean and clear, the trade group compliance officer or principal generally contacts the principal buyer directly.

The absolute Grade A+ method of showing Proof of Funds (POF) is for the client to provide a current Bank Tear Sheet (no older than 10 business days), showing adequate Funds and signed by Two Authorized Bank Officers. This is perhaps the fastest way to be accepted because, when signed, it is considered to be with full bank responsibility for Proof of Funds on the part of the Buyer's bank.

There has been a rash of fake bank-to-bank verifications that have caused the providers to take a hard stance about what they will accept as Proof of Funds (POF). They consider the signed tear sheet to be the gold standard for POF. Since they will deal only with the cream of the crop, a Client needs to follow the yellow brick road in order to get to the bank.

BUYER RELUCTANCE TO SHOW POF

Many Clients do not want their tear sheet exposed to prying eyes. In the Internet broker world, there is reason to fear. However, the reality is, IF you are dealing with the genuine and authentic people, there is NOTHING THAT ANYONE CAN DO WITH YOUR INFORMATION!

Do you truly believe your bank will allow someone to take or touch your account without contacting you to authorize it? In fact, if someone is that stupid to try to use the bank instrument that is in your name to relieve you of your funds, the bank will not only turn them away, but have them arrested for fraud. What a GREAT way to rid the world of these crooks.

However, the simplest and most effective solution that I recommend is to PASSWORD PROTECT the tear sheet after it is signed. Of course, you need to provide the password to the Provider's Rep so it can be reviewed. Once the provider's compliance officer receives Package 1, the first step is a first-round compliance check. This usually takes 24 to 48 hours (depending on the provider's workload). The provider's authorized officer then calls the buyer directly (principal to principal), to discuss the program and answer additional questions which can only be answered **after** the first check is done.

Once the bank receives the first package, THEY then call or email to the buyer directly and discuss his request. If all is ironed out in that call, the bank then prepares an Asset Management Agreement (also called the Trade Contract).

Until package 1 is received then, nothing can be sent back other than general information (*NOT an offer).

CHAPTER 4 - WHAT DOES "DUE DILIGENCE" MEAN?

An investigation or audit of a potential investment. Due diligence serves to confirm all material facts in regards to a sale or contract. Generally, due diligence refers to the care a reasonable person should take before entering into an agreement or a transaction with another party.

DUE DILIGENCE DEFINED - DD

1. Prior to participation in a trade program, favorable results of the due diligence analysis must occur. This includes reviewing all financial records plus anything else deemed material to the sale. Sellers could also perform a due diligence analysis on the buyer. Items that may be considered are the buyer's ability to purchase, as well as other items that would affect the purchased entity or the seller after the sale has been completed.

2. Due diligence is a way of preventing unnecessary harm to either party involved in a transaction

Two critical components of compliance fall under several different international definitions. The first piece of compliance relates to the Buyer Principal. Is he on a national or international black list (each bank and seller maintain their own internal black list which they will never reveal)?

Does he or she appear on the Specially Designated Nationals list from the US Treasury Office of Foreign Assets Control (OFAC)?

As it pertains to the world of banking, several rules and organizations dictate the requirements that each bank or provider must undertake before serving a client, such as:

"KNOW YOUR CLIENT/CUSTOMER"

Anti-money laundering now requires all financial institutions to verify new clients. KYC gives the institution, organization or bank the information they need to confirm an individual or company's existence and identify the individuals behind it, together with basic details about the company's credit worthiness. [1]

Now can you see there really IS a valid essential reason why a seller (whether a bank, licensed broker-dealer, or trader) must know who you are and where your money is located (*AND how you came to have it!)?

THE SIMPLE RULE IS:

No Proof of Funds and No Client Data = No Deal.

SOLICITATION/NON-SOLICITATION

We've already covered the reasons in this chapter. Suffice it to say, the evidence is in, and it is clear that the rules of engagement require that a potential transaction MUST start with the Client.

---

[1] Source: http://www.kycreports.co.uk/ In fact, a sample report might look like the one you will find at this link:
http://www.kycreports.co.uk/pdfs/productKYC.pdf
Source: http://www.bis.org/.

CHAPTER 4 - START THE CONVERSATION WITH THE PROVIDER

Now that you understand why the provider of any program MUST have you, as the Client, initiate the contact, there are some wrong ways, and one correct way to go about starting this process. Here, we focus on the right way to approach this.

PREPARE YOUR COMPLETE DOCUMENTATION

A common word term you will hear is "package". While this may not be a technical term to describe the contents that each buyer or client provides, it is useful to adopt the word as a short-hand expression. This is a compilation of the documents needed to begin the process.

As you have read, a legitimate provider cannot, or will not, open up a conversation with you until they know who you are exactly (via the Client Information Sheet and the Passport), and can also check on the legitimacy and authenticity of the money (your POF), you will use to enter into a program.

Bottom Line? YOU send the request for an invitation to the program first.

CHAPTER 5 - THE SUBMISSION

The receiving provider, once reviewed for completeness by the provider's point of contact, will open your initial documents. This first round of compliance takes anywhere from 24 to 48 hours on a good day. Sometimes faster. The initial documents that extend your introduction and desire to the provider are received and, after clearing the required compliance steps, the authorized principal contacts you directly. No intermediaries and in general no legal representatives ("Mandates", Powers of Attorney, "Appointed Representatives, etc.) are a party to this conversation. Only the specific principals will communicate from this point forward.

CHAPTER 6 - TIMELINES

Everyone wants it YESTERDAY! But the fact of the matter is there is a lot of machinery that goes to work behind the scenes, and eats up precious time.

Remember the story of The Tortoise and The Hare (or Rabbit- the point is, the moral is the same)?

The Hare or Rabbit, (or Hairy Rabbit??) starts the race with a bang... zooming away down the road, and leaving the Tortoise slowly plodding along. But the Hare runs out of steam soon, well before the finish line. While the Hare rested underneath a tree, the Tortoise had ploddingly loped along the road until he passed the sleeping Hare. By the time the Hare woke up to see the Tortoise -- just crossing the finish line-- it was too late! The Hare was in such a hurry, he ended up losing the race.

And so, it is in this world.

We are dealing in an arena which is part of the financial underpinnings of the world, where the select few are privileged to be invited in to the inner sanctum. That is why even this information is considered CONFIDENTIAL and only for the use of the Ultra High Net-Worth Individual or Corporate with the attitude and wherewithal needed to create a very private business relationship.

The sample graph below is a typical length of time for a transaction to move from start to finish. This is particularly true of an Unknown Buyer being introduced (After Package 1 has been submitted), to a seller who has never done business with him. Every transaction has a life-cycle of its own; some Clients who are already known to the

Seller can move much faster than this, others may have delaying problems that interfere, such as different time zones, or other factors.

The more information that you submit in Package 1, about you, your money, and your demonstration of being a good client of theirs, the sooner they will react. In this world at this time, this is a Seller's market. The Seller sets the procedures.

It seems arrogant in some ways, and I do not believe it is intentionally so. I think the business of the people in the back office is of such immense volume, the focus is lasered in on producing the work, rather than appearing to be concerned about helping a "Package Deficient" Buyer get it right. They are not in the business of teaching or nurturing new clients, and they are not trained to do so.

So, it falls to the Buyer to make certain that his Initial Package 1 is "right" and "tight". As a Buyer, the burden of proof falls on you, perhaps unfairly. However, the trick is to understand this environment, and creating the right package that contains EVERYTHING the Provider will want to see.

This is a Typical Timeline from Start to Finish for an actual, completed transaction. Notice that nothing happens in 1 day or 24 hours!
These times may be lengthened or shortened depending on the Client's responsiveness, the Bank's workload, or the Due Diligence.

STEP	Task Name	Duration
1	Client Submits CIS, LOR, Passport, POF	2d
2	Seller/Provider performs initial Due Diligence	2d
3	Provider contacts Buyer Principal directly	2d
4	Bank Desk produces full corporate offering documents	3d
5	Client completes all required FCO documents	1d
6	Bank Desk contacts Buyer Principal for last minute review	3d
7	Client executes final steps for Bank Desk	1d
8	Start of Trade: Generally Monday, Tuesday or Wednesday	2d 4h
9	Next Tranches Begin as Scheduled	1d

Figure 1 A timeline example for the processing of a Client

CHAPTER 7 - HOW IS MY MONEY PROTECTED FROM LOSS

Since the Investor's money is being used to obtain a credit line, and the credit line is the money being placed into a trade account to be shown as accessible to the Trader each time he trades, there is already a "firewall" which keeps the credit line and the asset underneath it (the Investor's cash) protected.

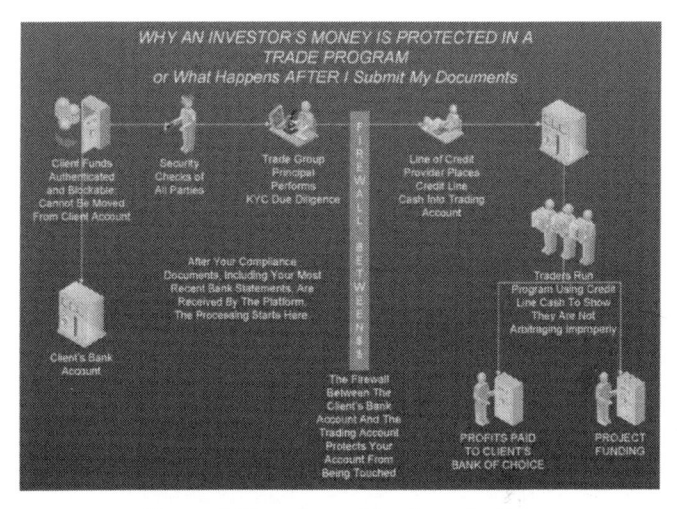

Figure 2 Flowchart of funds protection

CHAPTER 8 - SUMMARY

The intention in preparing this short guide for a very select few readers, is to help shed some light and alleviate some of the fears, (many rightfully deserved), of wasting time or being taken, or having their reputation sullied.

It has taken several years of crawling around the snakes and rats to recognize that the only thing that will make a transaction be successful, is when both the Principals are introduced in a good way, and can have a private discussion.

If there is a deal to be made, the atmosphere will have to be conducive. It will always depend on both the Client and the Provider being committed to provide what the other needs, and profiting in return.

I also recognize that some of the writings in this may offend some, whilst others will be nodding their heads in agreement. This publication is a compendium of direct experiences of the author. It is his opinion and judgment, based on participation and observation of the approaches that work, and many that don't.

If, by chance, someone has allowed an intermediary broker to read this document (shame on you!), then I hope it will provide a background for working in a better, professional manner. Although I am appalled at the behaviors by many brokers, there are others who are committed enough to learn about this business instead of bluffing their way through. I have been blessed to have found a few who have learned a better, more professional way, and are learning how to discover if someone is genuine, or even authorized, to discuss a transaction.

Thank you for reading. If this has helped clear the smoke and mirrors a little bit for you, I am glad. To quote the late Sy Syms, "AN EDUCATED CONSUMER IS OUR BEST CUSTOMER".

We hope that this publication will help give you a basic understanding of this business. Of course, we learned a long time ago that we don't know everything. If you discover a verifiable inaccuracy in this publication your constructive feedback is welcome. Our goal is to present accurate, timely and useful information to our clients and on behalf of those providers we are fortunate enough to be working with.

That is the spirit and intention in which this has been written.

APPENDIX

A sample set of document templates are <u>Written Request for Initial Documents</u> for general use and understanding.

Each provider may have his or her own preferred format, but the information that these samples ask for are fairly universal for a transactional relationship to begin.

No matter how much experience in this arena you may have, remember that the rules as well as the availability of these can change by the day. Rules that you thought were intact a year ago, or even a month ago, may have changed without you knowing it. Nothing is more embarrassing than firmly stating what you thought you knew, only to learn that something has changed.

NOTE: There will be other documentation sent to the Client once these have been processed. This is normal and expected, and should not be a surprise when asked.

CLIENT INFORMATION SHEET

Directions: This document must be completed in full. If a line item does not pertain then insert the term: "N/A" (non-applicable). If the Client is an Individual, complete all the same data without information requested of a corporate entity.

Corporate Information

Full Name of Corporation:

Date of Incorporation:

Incorporated in (City/State/Country):

Registration Number:

Board of Directors (Name & Title):

Officers (Name & Title):

Shareholders (List all shareholders owning more than 5 % of all outstanding shares of Corporation):

Location of Address: Registered Address (Corporation)

Full Name of Corporation:

Street Address:

City:

State:

Country:

Postal Code:

Location of Address: Mailing Address (Corporation)

Full Name of Corporation:
Street Address:
City:
State:
Country:
Postal Code:

Contact Information (Corporation)

Telephone Number:
Fax Number:
Mobile Number:
Email Address:

Financial Information (Corporation)
Annual Income of Corporation:
Liquid Assets of Corporation:
Net Worth of Corporation:
Investment Experience (in years) of Corporation:

Languages / Translator

Languages:
Does the Signatory speak English?
If No, Name of Translator:
Tel Number:
Email Address:

Legal Advisor

Full Name:
Company:
Address:
City:
State:
Country:
Postal Code:
Telephone Number:
Fax Number:
Email Address:

Bank Information (Corporate)

* Please attach copy of **current** account statement from bank, no older than 10 business days.

Bank Name (where funds are currently on deposit):

Street Address:
City:
State:
Country:
Postal Code:

Account Name:

Account Number:

Sort Code ABA No.:

SWIFT Code:

Account Signatory (1):

Account Signatory (2):

Bank Officer # 1 Name:

Bank Officer # 2 Name:

Telephone Number:

Fax Number:

Bank Officers (Bank Domain) Email Account:

Client Account where Profits to be paid

Bank Name:

Street Address:

City:

State:

Country:

Postal Code:

Account Name:

Account Number:

Sort Code ABA No.:

SWIFT Code:

Bank Officer Name:

Telephone Number:

Fax Number:

Personal Information of Officer(s) of Corporation / Passport Information (Please attach copy of corporate resolutions adopted by the Board of Directors appointing and authorizing said officer(s) to represent and legally bind the corporation)

Duplicate the section below for each Director.

First Name:

Middle Name:

Last Name:

Gender:

Date of Birth:

Social Security Number:

Country of Citizenship:

Languages:

Passport Information of Officers(s) of Corporation

Please attach copy of photo and signature page of passport

Passport Number:

Date of Issue:

Date of Expiry:

Issuing Authority:

Location of Address: Home-Legal Residence (Officer(s) of Corporation)

Full Name of Officer:

Street Address:

City:

State:

Country:

Postal Code:

(Below, duplicates the section above for each Director)

Investment

Funds available for this transaction:

Type of currency:

Origin of funds:

Are these funds free and clear of all liens, encumbrances and third-party interests?

I, **(NAME),** hereby swear under penalty of perjury, that the information provided herein is accurate and true as of this date, _____

For and on behalf of **(NAME OF COMPANY)**

Signature: _____ SEAL OF COMPANY

Name / Title:
Company:
Passport Number:
Date of Issue:
Date of Expiry:
Country of Issuance:

CORPORATE RESOLUTION – IF APPLICABLE

INVESTOR TRANSACTION CODE:

All of the directors of **(COMPANY NAME)** below listed were in attendance, in person or by telephone conference. General discussion was then held concerning the issue, and all aspects of the same, were fully explained in detail to the satisfaction of the board members.

DIRECTOR Name/Title:
Passport No.:

DIRECTOR Name/Title:
Passport No.:

DIRECTOR Name/Title:
Passport No.:

SECRETARY Name/Title:
Passport No.:

The Board of Directors of **(COMPANY NAME)** an International Business Company incorporated on **(DATE)** in **(LOCATION)** in **(COUNTRY)**, with Registered Offices at **(ADDRESS)** in a meeting held on this the **(Day)** Day of **(MONTH)**, **(YEAR)**, adopted the following resolutions.

RESOLUTION 1:

It is resolved that the Board of Directors of **(COMPANY NAME)** hereby appoints and authorizes its **(President-CEO etc.)**, **(NAME)**, holder of **(COUNTRY)** Passport Number **(NUMBER)** issued on **(DATE)**, as our Managing

Member to act with full authority on our behalf, stay and name, to instruct, negotiate, arrange, monitor, execute, manage and sign any and all agreements and/or necessary contracts with third parties pertinent to all financial transactions with bank instruments (securities/derivatives)

RESOLUTION 2:

It is resolved that at this meeting of the Board of Directors that our Managing Member and in fact **(NAME)** acts for **(COMPANY NAME)** with regards to the aforesaid financial investment.

RESOLUTION 3:

It is resolved that **(NAME)** is hereby authorized to act as our Financial Director for the aforesaid purpose.

RESOLUTION 4:

It is resolved the Board of Directors of **(COMPANY NAME)** hereby authorized **(NAME)** to assume all authority, powers, duties, signatory rights and responsibilities on our behalf.

RESOLUTION 5:

It is resolved that **(NAME)** is hereby authorized to open a personal, corporate, trading, trust and/or custodial account in any bank, domestic or foreign and to sign such resolutions as may be required by such bank to accomplish the objective(s) as stated herein and to give irrevocable instructions to said bank(s) on our behalf.

I, **(NAME)**, hereby swear under penalty of perjury, that the information provided herein is accurate and true as of this date: June 8, 2015

For and on behalf of **(NAME OF COMPANY)**

Signature: _____ SEAL OF COMPANY

Name / Title:

Company:

Passport Number:

Date of Issue:

Date of Expiry:

Country of Issuance:

Signature: _____

Name / Title: **SECRETARY**

Company:

Passport Number:

Date of Issue:

Date of Expiry:

Country of Issuance:

PASSPORT

PROVIDE COLOR COPY ENLARGED (140%) TO THIS SIZE (8½ X 11 INCHES). PICTURE MUST BE CLEAR AND NOT DARK. ENLARGE & LIGHTEN (USING PHOTO SETTING). COLOR SCAN THE PASSPORT INTO YOUR COMPUTER AT A HIGH RESOLUTION IN THE JPEG FORMAT AND INSERT.

PROOF OF FUNDS

CURRENT BANK STATEMENT

CURRENT BANK STATEMENT OR RECENT TEAR SHEET IS THE REQUESTED ACCEPTABLE PROOF OF FUNDS. BCL, BANK LETTERS SIGNED BY BANK OFFICER(S), CERTIFICATE OF ACCOUNT OR CONFIRMATION OF FUNDS MAY BE INCLUDED AS SUPPLEMENTAL BANKING VERIFICATION. KINDLY INCLUDE UN-SANITIZED CURRENT BANK STATEMENT OR TEAR SHEET WITH YOUR SUBMISSION. TRANSMIT HIGH-QUALITY, COLOR SCANS OF REAL DOCUMENTS. THANK YOU. MOST IMPORTANT IS TO SHOW ACTUAL CASH AMOUNT SITTING IN THE ACCOUNT, AS IT WILL BE VERIFIED.

Made in the USA
Las Vegas, NV
23 September 2021